COPYBOOK III

Manuscript

Scripture & Poems

Cheryl Lowe & Leigh Lowe

MEMORIA PRESS

MEMORIA PRESS
www.MemoriaPress.com

COPYBOOK III
Manuscript

SCRIPTURE & POEMS
Cheryl Lowe & Leigh Lowe

ISBN 978-1-61538-583-6

Table of Contents

INTRODUCTION

What is copybook?

Copybook is a time-honored learning activity in which students copy Scripture, maxims, poetry and other literature selections. Copybook, like memorization, is a forgotten skill in modern education. However, like memorization, copybook is a beginning skill that is indispensable to the development of good language skills.

What important skills are practiced in copybook? In copybook, students practice penmanship, spelling, reading comprehension, punctuation, and vocabulary. Students develop the habits of accuracy, neatness, attention to detail, and patience; they practice correct grammar and good writing style; they develop an appreciation for what is good, noble, and beautiful in literature.

Copybook is not the only way for the young student to practice each of these skills—but it is the only exercise that develops all of them at the same time. Copybook is concrete and physical; it complements and completes the mental exercise of memorization and reading. Copybook is so simple and obvious that we overlook it.

Even though penmanship is hard work for the young student, he should come to delight in the physical act of creating a beautiful page of writing. Because the student is not burdened by trying to compose his own words, he is liberated to concentrate on copying the immortal words of others. The young student who is not able to think great thoughts of his own can grow in wisdom by thinking great thoughts of others. And as a reward for completing his copybook exercise he can illustrate the words he has copied with his own drawing. After the discipline of copybook he can exercise his imagination and creativity; the original drawings of children are the perfect companion to copybook.

How did we select our Bible verses?

The King James Bible is the poetic and literary version of Scripture. It has had a tremendous influence on the development of the English language. Many spiritual and literary allusions and expressions come directly from the King James Bible. A thorough knowledge of the King James Bible is a necessary preparation for the study of English literature, as well as a foundation for a deep spiritual life.

Because memorization is a lost art, parents and teachers today rarely have a vision for the quantity and quality of Scripture and poetry that children can and should commit to memory. The selection of passages is important in that they should lead the young child into a love and appreciation for Scripture; they should be age-appropriate passages, ones that employ poetic language to paint concrete pictures of Bible stories. Verses in our K-2 Copybooks focus on the great dramatic stories in salvation history rather than on doctrinal or abstract concepts, which are best reserved for the more mature student.

The K-2 Copybook memory verses are reviewed in the Memoria Press Christian Studies program for grades 3-6. The goal is for students to memorize and retain all of the Scripture they have learned over the course of their entire school years so that each year they can recite all of the verses from the current year plus all from previous years. A complete Bible memorization program allows for the student to absorb a vast body of Scripture of great variety and content over the whole of the Bible.

TEACHING GUIDELINES

The first task of the teacher is to communicate the importance of the lesson to the student and to model enthusiasm. The child should see copybook as an opportunity to give his very best effort in penmanship and artwork throughout the year. Students should be inspired to produce quality work because the words they are asked to memorize and copy are often the sacred words of Scripture. The quality of the work will be a direct reflection of the ability of the teacher to motivate the child to excellence.

In this third book of the Copybook series, the student will focus his copying effort on managing a blank page. Words are not modeled for the child as in Copybooks I and II, and the line spacing is smaller to help the child transition to regular notebook paper. Special attention should be given to vertical margins and word spacing. We suggest that the student limit lines to four or five words each. Students should also begin learning syllabication. If a word must be divided between two lines, the student should be required to divide the word properly between two syllables.

The Copybook Lesson outlined below need not be done in one sitting, but may be broken up into several sessions.

Step 1 ______________________________

Bible Story Time. Write the memory verse on the board. Read the verse from a Bible. A traditional soft leather Bible is best because it communicates better that the Bible is a special book, the sacred Word of God. Keep the Bible in your room or home in a special place and handle it with reverence. You will want to read the context of the verse from the Bible and/or from a story book. We recommend *The Golden Children's Bible* because its words are closest to Scripture and because the pictures are realistic and memorable.

Step 2 ______________________________

Language Lesson. Using the blackboard, study the verse with students. Identify unfamiliar words and explain their meanings in context, rather than by using the dictionary. Scripture and poetry often contain archaic or poetic words that are not common in contemporary writing, words such as "thee," "thy," "giveth," "firmament," etc. Children are intrigued by these "interesting words" and early exposure to them enriches their language education. Even though Scripture and poetry may also have non-standard punctuation and grammar, the passages can be used to introduce simple grammar topics: nouns, verbs, punctuation, capitalization, plurals, contractions, etc.

Step 3 ______________________________

Memorization. Use the disappearing line technique. Recite the whole verse together several times. Break the verse down into small sections. Have students recite one section together, and then erase that section. Pointing to the "erased" section on the board, ask students individually and then in unison to recite what you erased. Repeat until the whole verse has been erased from the board. (Knowing the words are going to be erased helps students concentrate and adds excitement.) By the end of the process, students will be able to repeat the whole verse from memory. For instance, for the first passage the three sections would be:

And God said,
"Let there be light":
and there was light.

Step 4 ____

Copying. Now that students are familiar with the verse, they copy it on the lined, facing page in their best handwriting. It is critical that students develop correct techniques for managing a blank page. This includes obeying margins, spacing words properly, and dividing words according to syllabication rules. The teacher should monitor students during copybook time and quickly correct any errors. The great value of copybook is that, unlike all of the other writing students do, copybook is a special time for students to give their very best effort.

Step 5 ____

Proofreading and Correction. Students should proof and correct all work. This is a critical skill that must be taught, encouraged, and practiced from the beginning of the child's education. The proofreading should be kept as a separate exercise and have sufficient time devoted to it. The lesson is not complete until this exercise of proofreading and correction produces a "finished" product.

Step 6 ____

Illustration. Students can now draw a picture to illustrate the Bible verse or poem. Help students to include as many details as possible. Art brings the copybook exercise to a close with delight and imagination. These drawings will be cherished in years to come.

Step 7 ____

Review. Part of every lesson should be devoted to a review of verses learned, both in this book and in *Copybook I* and *II.* Students love to practice what they already know. Give students the first word or two of each passage, and let them complete the passage as a group recitation or individually. As the verses accumulate, students will be amazed at what they know and will develop confidence in their abilities. At the end of the year students should be able to recite all verses with fluency.

Recommended Schedule

Please see complete instructions for each step on previous pages.

Day 1: Step One - Bible Story Time (15 min.)

Day 2: Step Two - Language Lesson (15 min.)

Day 3: Steps Three & Four - Memorization and Copying (20 min.)

Day 4: Steps Five & Seven - Proofreading and Cumulative Review of all Memory Work (15-30 min)

Day 5: Step Six - Illustration (20 min.)

Week 1	Genesis 1:1-5, Part I
Week 2	Genesis 1:1-5, Part II
Week 3	Genesis 2:7
Week 4	Genesis 2:18
Week 5	Genesis 2:23-24
Week 6	Genesis 6:8-10
Week 7	Genesis 27:22
Week 8	Exodus 3:6
Week 9	I Samuel 17:26
Week 10	Matthew 2:1-2
Week 11	Matthew 2:11
Week 12	Matthew 25:35-36
Week 13	Matthew 25:40
Week 14	Matthew 7:7
Week 15	Matthew 7:20, Matthew 19:30
Week 16	Matthew 26:41
Week 17	Revelation 22:13
Week 18	Books of the Old Testament, Part I
Week 19	Books of the Old Testament, Part II
Week 20	Books of the Old Testament, Part III
Week 21	Twelve Tribes of Israel
Week 22	Psalm 23, Part I
Week 23	Psalm 23, Part II
Week 24	Psalm 23, Part III
Week 25	All Things Bright and Beautiful
Week 26	All Things Bright and Beautiful
Week 27	In the Fields
Week 28	In the Fields
Week 29	The Flowers
Week 30	The Flowers
Week 31	Let Dogs Delight to Bark and Bite
Week 32	Let Dogs Delight to Bark and Bite

Line and Letter Practice

We have found that little instruction is necessary to teach basic letter strokes. Instead, it is "practice, practice, practice" on words and passages that creates neat and proficient writers. The following page, however, can be used to reinforce letter formation that may prove problematic. You may use these exercises to practice strokes and letters before beginning copy work. If your student does not need focused practice on creating individual letters, you may skip this section and move straight to the first Bible verse.

Letter Practice Overview

Start with basic vertical, horizontal, slanted, and circular strokes. Do not underestimate a young student's ability to create simple strokes and stay within the lines. Always encourage straight lines, round circles, and appropriately sized letters. Once the basic strokes are mastered, your student should be able to make every letter in the alphabet. Each letter includes numbered stroke instruction. Many letters are created in a single continuous stroke where the student retraces his previous path.

Examples: np

Other letters require two or more strokes and each stroke will be numbered in sequence:

Examples: fI

It is not necessary to practice each letter over and over until it is perfect, just until your student has the basic ability to form letters correctly. The purpose of copybook is to allow your student to practice handwriting on great passages, not lists of letters. You will notice significant improvements in letter formation as the year progresses.

Remember, there are several different methods of creating letters. If your child has learned another system that works for him, skip the letter formation review section and move right into the copy work.

Student Guidelines

1. Students should hold pencils properly.

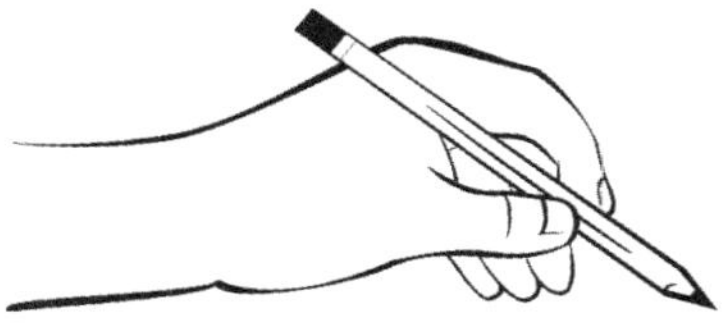

Left-handed

Right-handed

2. Start each line close to the left margin and don't cross the right margin.
3. Uppercase letters must touch the top and bottom lines.
4. Most lowercase letters start at the middle, dashed line.
5. Lowercase b, d, f, h, k, t, and l are all tall letters that touch the top line.
6. Lowercase g, j, p, q, and y have hooks or tails that cross the bottom line.
7. All words should be one pinky space apart.
8. Letters should all stand tall and straight.
9. Erase mistakes completely and be neat.

A B C D E

F G H I J

K L M N O

P Q R S T

U V W X Y Z

a b c d e

f g h i j

k l m n o

p q r s t

u v w x y z

Aa Bb Cc Dd Ee

Ff Gg Hh Ii Jj

Kk Ll Mm Nn Oo

Pp Qq Rr Ss Tt

Uu Vv Ww Xx Yy Zz

In the beginning God created
the heaven and the earth.
And the earth was without form, and void;
and darkness was upon the face of the deep.
And the Spirit of God
moved upon the face of the waters.
And God said, "Let there be light":
and there was light.

Genesis 1:1–5, Part I

Students may need two pages to copy this passage. Page 19 is also available.

In the beginning God created
the heaven and the earth.
And the earth was without form, and void;
and darkness was upon the face of the deep.
And the Spirit of God
moved upon the face of the waters.
And God said, "Let there be light":
and there was light.

Genesis 1:1–5, Part I

And God saw the light,
and it was good:
and God divided the light
from the darkness.
And God called the light Day,
and the darkness He called Night.
And the evening and the morning
were the first day.

Genesis 1:1–5, Part II

Students may need two pages to copy this passage. Page 23 is also available.

And God saw the light,
and it was good:
and God divided the light
from the darkness.
And God called the light Day,
and the darkness He called Night.
And the evening and the morning
were the first day.

Genesis 1:1–5, Part II

And the Lord God formed man
of the dust of the ground,
and breathed into his nostrils
the breath of life;
and man became a living soul.

Genesis 2:7

And the Lord God said,
"It is not good that man should be alone.
I will make a help meet for him."

Genesis 2:18

And Adam said,
"This is now bone of my bones,
and flesh of my flesh;
she shall be called Woman,
because she was taken out of Man."
Therefore shall a man leave
his father and his mother,
and shall cleave unto his wife;
and they shall be one flesh.

Genesis 2:23–24

Students may need two pages to copy this passage. Page 31 is also available.

And Adam said,
"This is now bone of my bones,
and flesh of my flesh;
she shall be called Woman,
because she was taken out of Man."
Therefore shall a man leave
his father and his mother,
and shall cleave unto his wife;
and they shall be one flesh.

Genesis 2:23–24

But Noah found grace
in the eyes of the Lord.
Noah was a just man
and perfect in his generation,
and Noah walked with God.
And Noah begat three sons,
Shem, Ham, and Japheth.

Genesis 6: 8–10

"The voice is Jacob's voice
but the hands are the hands of Esau."

Genesis 27:22

"I am the God of thy father,
the God of Abraham,
the God of Isaac,
and the God of Jacob."
And Moses hid his face;
for he was afraid to look upon God.

Exodus 3:6

"Who is this uncircumcised Philistine,
that he should defy the armies
of the living God?"

I Samuel 17:26

Now when Jesus was born
in Bethlehem of Judea
in the days of Herod the king,
behold, there came wise men
from the east to Jerusalem, saying,
"Where is He that is born King of the Jews?
For we have seen His star in the east,
and are come to worship Him."
Matthew 2:1–2

Students may need two pages to copy this passage. Page 43 is also available.

Now when Jesus was born
in Bethlehem of Judea
in the days of Herod the king,
behold, there came wise men
from the east to Jerusalem, saying,
"Where is He that is born King of the Jews?
For we have seen His star in the east,
and are come to worship Him."

Matthew 2:1–2

They saw the young Child
with Mary His mother,
and fell down, and worshipped Him:
and when they had opened their treasures,
they presented unto Him gifts;
gold, frankincense, and myrrh.

Matthew 2:11

"For I was hungry and you gave Me food.
I was thirsty and you gave Me drink.
I was a stranger, and you took Me in.
I was naked and you clothed Me.
I was sick and you visited Me.
I was in prison and you came to Me."

Matthew 25:35–36

"Inasmuch as you have done it
to one of the least of these My brethren,
you have done it unto Me."

Matthew 25:40

"Ask, and it shall be given you;
seek and ye shall find;
knock and it shall be opened unto you."

Matthew 7:7

"By their fruits ye shall know them."

Matthew 7:20

"Many that are first shall be last;
and the last shall be first."

Matthew 19:30

"Father, if Thou be willing,
remove this cup from Me:
nevertheless, not My will,
but Thine, be done."

Luke 22:42

"Watch and pray,
that you enter not into temptation:
the spirit indeed is willing,
but the flesh is weak."

Matthew 26:41

"I am the Alpha and the Omega,
the Beginning and the End,
the First and the Last."

Revelation 22:13

Books of the Old Testament, Part I

Genesis
Exodus
Leviticus
Numbers
Deuteronomy
Joshua
Judges
Ruth
I Samuel
II Samuel
I Kings
II Kings
I Chronicles
II Chronicles

Books of the Old Testament, Part II

Ezra
Nehemiah
Esther
Job
Psalms
Proverbs
Ecclesiastes
The Song of Solomon
Isaiah
Jeremiah
Lamentations
Ezekiel

Books of the Old Testament, Part III

Daniel
Hosea
Joel
Amos
Obadiah
Jonah
Micah

Nahum
Habakkuk
Zephaniah
Haggai
Zechariah
Malachi

Twelve Tribes of Israel

Reuben	Benjamin
Simeon	Dan
Levi	Naphtali
Judah	Gad
Issachar	Asher
Zebulun	Joseph

The Lord is my shepherd; I shall not want.
He maketh me to lie down in green pastures:
He leadeth me beside the still waters,
He restoreth my soul:
He leadeth me in the paths
of righteousness for His name's sake.

Psalm 23, Part I

Yea, though I walk through the valley
of the shadow of death,
I will fear no evil: for Thou art with me;
Thy rod and Thy staff they comfort me.
Thou preparest a table before me
in the presence of mine enemies.

Psalm 23, Part II

Thou anointest my head with oil;
my cup runneth over.
Surely goodness and mercy
shall follow me all the days of my life:
and I will dwell in the house
of the Lord forever.

Psalm 23, Part III

All Things Bright and Beautiful

By Cecil F. Alexander

All things bright and beautiful,
All creatures great and small,
All things wise and wonderful:
The Lord God made them all.

Each little flower that opens,
Each little bird that sings,
He made their glowing colors,
He made their tiny wings.

The purple headed mountains,
The river running by,
The sunset and the morning
That brightens up the sky.

The cold wind in the winter,
The pleasant summer sun,
The ripe fruits in the garden:
God made them every one.

He gave us eyes to see them,
And lips that we might tell
How great is God Almighty,
Who has made all things well.

Students may need two or three pages to copy this poem. Pages 79 and 81 are also available. The drawing pages are on pages 82 and 83.

All Things Bright and Beautiful

By Cecil F. Alexander

All things bright and beautiful,
All creatures great and small,
All things wise and wonderful:
The Lord God made them all.

Each little flower that opens,
Each little bird that sings,
He made their glowing colors,
He made their tiny wings.

The purple headed mountains,
The river running by,
The sunset and the morning
That brightens up the sky.

The cold wind in the winter,
The pleasant summer sun,
The ripe fruits in the garden:
God made them every one.

He gave us eyes to see them,
And lips that we might tell
How great is God Almighty,
Who has made all things well.

All Things Bright and Beautiful

By Cecil F. Alexander

All things bright and beautiful,
All creatures great and small,
All things wise and wonderful:
The Lord God made them all.

Each little flower that opens,
Each little bird that sings,
He made their glowing colors,
He made their tiny wings.

The purple headed mountains,
The river running by,
The sunset and the morning
That brightens up the sky.

The cold wind in the winter,
The pleasant summer sun,
The ripe fruits in the garden:
God made them every one.

He gave us eyes to see them,
And lips that we might tell
How great is God Almighty,
Who has made all things well.

In the Fields

Unknown

The little cares that fretted me,
I lost them yesterday,
Among the fields, above the sea,
Among the winds at play;
Among the lowing of the herds,
The rustling of the trees;
Among the singing of the birds,
The humming of the bees.

The foolish fears of what might pass,
I cast them all away,
Among the clover scented grass,
Among the new mown hay;
Among the husking of the corn
Where drowsy poppies nod,
Where ill thoughts die and good are born,
Out in the fields of God.

Students may need two pages to copy this poem. Page 87 is also available. The drawing pages are on pages 88 and 89.

In the Fields

Unknown

The little cares that fretted me,
I lost them yesterday,
Among the fields, above the sea,
Among the winds at play;
Among the lowing of the herds,
The rustling of the trees;
Among the singing of the birds,
The humming of the bees.

The foolish fears of what might pass,
I cast them all away,
Among the clover scented grass,
Among the new mown hay;
Among the husking of the corn
Where drowsy poppies nod,
Where ill thoughts die and good are born,
Out in the fields of God.

The Flowers

Robert Louis Stevenson

All the names I know from nurse:
Gardener's garters, Shepherd's purse,
Bachelor's buttons, Lady's smock,
And, the Lady Hollyhock.

Fairy places, fairy things,
Fairy woods where the wild bee wings,
Tiny trees for tiny dames—
These must all be fairy names!

Tiny woods below whose boughs
Shady fairies weave a house;
Tiny tree tops, rose or thyme,
Where the braver fairies climb!

Fair are grown up people's trees,
But the fairest woods are these;
Where if I were not so tall,
I should live for good and all.

Students may need two or three pages to copy this poem. Pages 93 and 95 are also available.
The drawing pages are on pages 96 and 97.

The Flowers

Robert Louis Stevenson

All the names I know from nurse:
Gardener's garters, Shepherd's purse,
Bachelor's buttons, Lady's smock,
And, the Lady Hollyhock.

Fairy places, fairy things,
Fairy woods where the wild bee wings,
Tiny trees for tiny dames--
These must all be fairy names!

Tiny woods below whose boughs
Shady fairies weave a house;
Tiny tree tops, rose or thyme,
Where the braver fairies climb!

Fair are grown up people's trees,
But the fairest woods are these;
Where if I were not so tall,
I should live for good and all.

The Flowers

Robert Louis Stevenson

All the names I know from nurse:
Gardener's garters, Shepherd's purse,
Bachelor's buttons, Lady's smock,
And, the Lady Hollyhock.

Fairy places, fairy things,
Fairy woods where the wild bee wings,
Tiny trees for tiny dames--
These must all be fairy names!

Tiny woods below whose boughs
Shady fairies weave a house;
Tiny tree tops, rose or thyme,
Where the braver fairies climb!

Fair are grown up people's trees,
But the fairest woods are these;
Where if I were not so tall,
I should live for good and all.

Let Dogs Delight to Bark and Bite

Isaac Watts

Let dogs delight to bark and bite,
For God has made them so;
Let bears and lions growl and fight,
For 'tis their nature, too.

But, children, you should never let
Such angry passions rise;
Your little hands were never made
To tear each other's eyes.

Let love through all your actions run,
And all your words be mild;
Live like the blessed Virgin's Son,
That sweet and lovely child.

His soul was gentle as a lamb;
And as His stature grew,
He grew in favor both with man
And God His Father, too.

Now, Lord of all, He reigns above;
And from His heavenly throne,
He sees what children dwell in love,
And marks them for His own.

Students may need two or three pages to copy this poem. Pages 101 and 103 are also available.
The drawing pages are on pages 104 and 105.

Let Dogs Delight to Bark and Bite

Isaac Watts

Let dogs delight to bark and bite,
For God has made them so;
Let bears and lions growl and fight,
For 'tis their nature, too.

But, children, you should never let
Such angry passions rise;
Your little hands were never made
To tear each other's eyes.

Let love through all your actions run,
And all your words be mild;
Live like the blessed Virgin's Son,
That sweet and lovely child.

His soul was gentle as a lamb;
And as His stature grew,
He grew in favor both with man
And God His Father, too.

Now, Lord of all, He reigns above;
And from His heavenly throne,
He sees what children dwell in love,
And marks them for His own.

Let Dogs Delight to Bark and Bite

Isaac Watts

Let dogs delight to bark and bite,
For God has made them so;
Let bears and lions growl and fight,
For 'tis their nature, too.

But, children, you should never let
Such angry passions rise;
Your little hands were never made
To tear each other's eyes.

Let love through all your actions run,
And all your words be mild;
Live like the blessed Virgin's Son,
That sweet and lovely child.

His soul was gentle as a lamb;
And as His stature grew,
He grew in favor both with man
And God His Father, too.

Now, Lord of all, He reigns above;
And from His heavenly throne,
He sees what children dwell in love,
And marks them for His own.

Spare Drawing & Copy Sheets

(Reproducible)